MEOPHAM
CHANGING PLACES

MEOPHAM HISTORICAL SOCIETY

FONTHILL

Fonthill Media Limited
www.fonthillmedia.com
office@fonthillmedia.com

First published in the United Kingdom 2014

British Library Cataloguing in Publication Data:
A catalogue record for this book is available from the British Library

ISBN 978-1-78155-125-7

Typeset in Mrs Eaves XL Serif Nar OT
Printed and bound in England

Introduction

The original concept for this publication was to prepare a reprint of the *Meopham in Old Picture Postcards* book (affectionately known as the Blue Book because of its colour) published in 1986 and produced by our local historian and past President of the Meopham Historical Society, Jim Carley. On later consideration by the Historical Society, it was realised that the addition of matching contemporary photographs of the same sites and buildings would attract increasing local interest. As Meopham is such an historic village in so many ways, it was thought important to include as many old buildings as could be accommodated in a single publication. This has now been achieved in this edition of *Meopham Changing Places* which will take its place in the series showing changes over the years in English villages. It is to be dedicated to the memory of Jim Carley who loved and researched this village for most of his life.

I have received considerable help from members of our Society, past and present, who have assisted in research or have taken photographs for me. I owe a huge debt to Jim Carley because almost one half of the Old Meopham pictures have come from his publication as have the accompanying historical captions. Several of his other books have helped me with the historical detail which I have added here. I am also indebted to Joan Goodwins, current President of the Society, for her generous help in sharing with me her extensive knowledge of old Meopham and for her expertise in editing the manuscript. Many members and friends have lent old pictures or have taken contemporary photographs for me, among them are Maureen Arrowsmith, Keith Boxall, Colin Greene, Doug Grierson, and Ann Kneif. I am very grateful to them all and apologise to any whose names have been accidentally omitted. Finally, I accept personally full responsibility for what you are about to read and hope you enjoy it.

John Trethewey
(Past chairman Meopham Historical Society)

A SIMPLIFIED MAP OF MEOPHAM

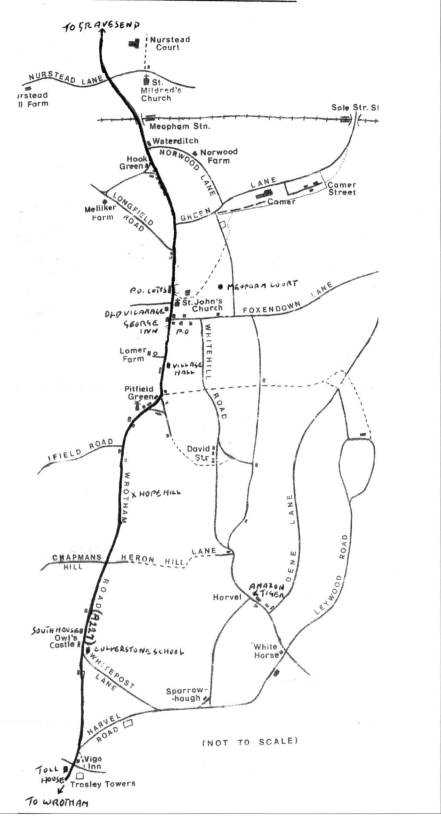

The railway through Meopham was built by the London, Chatham & Dover Railway Company in 1860 and Meopham station was opened to traffic in May 1861. The original wooden buildings of the passenger station are seen here, and they survived in this form for about 110 years. The original train service was about four or five times a day to London and the same number in the down direction, most of them continuing their journey along the Kent coast through Canterbury to Dover. The station was a point of call for the horse bus route operated by Mr Clark from Meopham Green to Gravesend, and his bus is seen here at the station entrance in the old picture. Car parking is now confined to the adjacent parking area except in the case of temporary parking as can be seen in the modern picture.

The former grocery stores that stood at the junction of Station Road and Wrotham Road were destroyed by fire in 1890. Here we see the proprietor, Mr Herbert Johnson, ruefully surveying the debris. The only thing that seems to have survived is the facia board, containing advertisement for Dr Ridge's patent medicine. Station Road is on the left, at that time containing fewer houses. Those on the left of the road were built to house railway workers, and for a long time were called Railway Cottages. Beyond them were green fields. The shop property was rebuilt after the fire, in the form in which we now know it. This business was later taken over by Mr V. Mackley who moved down from his shop shown on page 11 and is now occupied by Kings Estate Agents.

Railway Approach, Meopham.

This view dates from the early years of this century. The public house is seen in a stage of transition. The name painted onto the front wall calls it the Railway Hotel, but careful scrutiny of the hanging sign shows the change of name to the one now in use, The Railway Tavern. The advert on the front wall is for G. Masters & Co. of New Road, Gravesend, and carries the traditional picture of a pantechnicon, used by all removal contractors at that time. These vehicles had small wheels, could be run onto a flat railway wagon for long distance transport, and so performed the same function as do containers today. Coming up out of the station yard is a one-horse coal cart, and a cab can be seen waiting for custom in front of the station buildings. The station and the forecourt were lit by oil lamps and it was the duty of the junior member of the station staff to see that they were properly filled and trimmed. The modern picture shows the pub as it is today.

This view of Wrotham Road, looking South from the Railway Tavern, taken in the 1920s shows the wool, drapery and gift shop known as Gay Cousins. This corrugated-roofed building originally housed a small private school and was used for occasional entertainments. It thrived as a shop from the 1950s to the late 1970s but was eventually demolished, together with an adjoining large disused garage, and replaced by two contemporary private houses. The small traffic island was not yet created, nor was the road asphalted and the ten pairs of telegraph wires are evidence of the slow growth of the telephone system. The latest picture shows how the road has been made wider in keeping with the increased flow of traffic.

This photograph of a Meopham garage dates from the 1920s, it was replaced in the 1960s by another garage, also on the west side of Wrotham Road, owned by an Indian Sikh family. But in 1980, the site was sold to developers and the garage demolished. Subsequently the two Sunningdale Court apartment buildings were erected on the same site, as shown, and these soon became occupied.

Nevill Place, Meopham.

The name Nevill is spelt without the final 'e' in Meopham. James Carley thought that this was due to some distant connection with Lord Abergavenny, whose family name it is. Mr Carley goes on to explain, in his booklet *Meopham at Work at Play and at Prayer* that Number 1 Nevill Place was formerly a general store and post office. The latter was then moved to Number 2 and combined with the newsagent function. The new picture shows that the main changes are the shops, the road width and the introduction of bollards.

This picture, dating from about 1910, shows the shops on the east side of Wrotham Road just south of the station. The white houses in the centre were then, according to contemporary legal documents, 'two semi-detached dwelling houses called Nevill Villas situated near Meopham Railway Station', and owned by the French family. The left-hand one was converted into the post office and general store, with the right-hand one being the postmaster's house. The creeper-covered house next to them remains minus the creeper, as a private house. The shops next to them were owned by Henry Bishop, grocery and provision dealer. He died in 1901, and his executors sold the entire property to William Norton, the miller at Meopham Green, for £750. As will be seen by the fascia board, he traded there as J. & W. Norton. The left-hand shop, now the newsagent, was leased to W. G. Aldridge, with a covenant against selling anything that the Nortons were likely to sell. In 1906 Aldridge sold out to Mr V. Mackley, who later moved to the premises at Station Road his shop bearing the logo, 'Enquire within for Everything' (see photograph on page 6). Norton's shops are now occupied by Charisma and the baker as shown.

This building was bought from the Nortons in 1930 by Cyril and Roland King and became a butchery. In the doorway are Roland King and his assistant 'Sonny' Hollman. Mr Hollman remained with the firm throughout his working life, and still, after some years of retirement, was sometimes to be seen in the shop. The motorcycle with the two attached lidded boxes was used for all deliveries, non-refrigerated! Cyril's second son, Brian, took over the shop on the death of his father in 1972 and ran it until closure in 1990. The interior of the shop has changed little over the years, the stable-door being retained as has the cashier's 'throne-till' and cashier's office. A carcass of meat can be seen hanging behind the door, in the area where customers used to wait to be served. There was little refrigeration then. The shop is now owned by Charisma which has extended its premises to cover the second section of the bakery.

The growth of the village after the First World War led to the need for more shops, and this block of three was built on the west side of Wrotham Road about 1930. They faced the earlier shops shown on page 6. At first only two were let, Mr Marshall, our first resident estate agent, offered pieces of land, probably in three newly laid out roads at the back of the shops, as well as houses for sale and to let. The centre shop doubled as a post office and a café. The post office later crossed the road. Subsequently the estate office became a branch of Midland Bank, and the other two the local co-op. In 1980, these were demolished and turned into the block of flats known as Nevill Court. The modern picture shows how this is now a residential building.

These pictures show Waterditch Corner named after the Waterditch building adjacent to the north as shown on page 15. This corner is at the junction of the Wrotham Road and Norwood Lane to the east, the latter known for the presence of a well about 400 feet deep in days gone by. On the south side of the corner is Arborfield once the residence and surgery of Dr Hasler. Subsequently, but before the erection of the Meopham Health Centre surgery, the village surgery was situated at Homefield which was further to the south on the eastern side of the Wrotham Road now demolished and replaced by two contemporary houses.

Waterditch was originally six farm labourers' cottages, including a forge, and is presumed to be the oldest building in the village. Ancient maps of Meopham show the existence of roadside ponds which used to collect surface water, as water was a scarce commodity. This helped to refresh cattle and sheep while being driven through the village and evidence of the local collection of water after heavy rain can be seen in the picture on page 16. It is therefore not surprising that a building in an area occupied by a pond was named Waterditch. The building is now occupied as a single residence.

As explained in the caption on page 15, this is one of the original pond sites and water does tend to lie in this area, even to this day in spite of the gallant efforts of the parish and the county councils.

Hilton Villa was the house of the local coal merchant, Mr F. C. Judson who operated the coal trade in Meopham at the end of the nineteenth century. The firm later became Judson & Fletcher, who continued in business until quite recently, supplies being delivered by road after 1962. Frank Judson generously donated the ground behind his house for the play area which became known as the Judson Recreation Ground, as well as the smaller parcel of land known as Gunn's Field which was given to the local Boy Scouts.

Here we have a view of the north end of Hook Green when a signpost was in position and before the installation of the Meopham sign in the later picture, shown more clearly in the photograph on page 19. The road leading to the west of the Wrotham Road, and following the western edge of Hook Green, is Melliker Lane.

These pictures show a view of the south end of Hook Green, before and after the installation of the Meopham sign. The sign was designed by a member of the Meopham Historical Society, Mr Eric Bugg, and placed in position in 1998. It depicts important features of the history of Meopham, such as the Windmill and the tradition of cricket on the green since 1776, highlighted by the cricket stumps, ball and bat. The Tradescantia plant showing Meopham's relationship with the gardener to King Charles I, John Tradescant, who married a Meopham girl in the church of St John the Baptist and whose son was christened there. The Bishop's mitre represents the election of Simon de Meopham, a local lad, as Archbishop of Canterbury in 1328.

The well-wooded picture of the main road at Hook Green gives perhaps a deceptive view of the width of the road about 1930. The entrance on the extreme left leads to Waterditch Cottage, as shown on page 15. The long wooden fence has been replaced by a well-cut hedge. Near the cyclist is the junction with Norwood Lane, leading past Norwood Farm to Camer. On the far side of this road is Arborfield, shown more clearly in the later photograph, for many years the residence of Dr W. D. Hasler, the village doctor, but after his death converted into a number of flats. Further on, the road has now been widened, and several of the trees have been lost in the process including the pine trees after which Pine Close was named.

Weaver's Cottage, as we call it today was originally one of four pairs of cottages built about 1832 to house the poor who could no longer be accommodated by the parish workhouse. Firstly roofed by thatch and known as the Hook Green Cottages, by the end of the century the cottages had been converted to one dwelling and this was described as 'formerly a knitting factory'. Also part of the building was used as a school. Note the four trees, behind the cottage. These are part of a group of trees planted to commemorate Queen Victoria's Diamond Jubilee in 1897. The jubilee trees, seen also in the modern picture, are in excellent condition in spite of their age.

Melliker Green is situated at the junction of Longfield Road and Melliker Lane, and is one of the smallest of the village greens. This picture was taken some time before 1925, when Longfield Road was widened to take modern traffic. The gnarled yew tree stands on the north side of the green, and is here seen in a rather sorry state. Fires had been lit in the hollow trunk, and it looked as though its end was near. However in 1928 the parish council erected a fence round it, and it stands today in very good condition as can be seen in the 'now' picture. The field behind the tree is occupied by a modern farmhouse appropriately called Three Ways. The gate to the left led to a public footpath to Longfield Hill, the route of which was incorporated into the new road. The name Melliker is derived from the Old English *Myldenakre* meaning roughly 'at the soft cultivated piece of land'.

The Fox and Hounds public house lies just south of Hook Green. The earliest record can be found in the Rate book of 1836, when it was a beer house run by George French. The original building, which survived until 1924, was three stories high but was then replaced by the existing building which has since been extended. A 1903 advert decreed that the pub sold ales and stout from the Dartford Brewery and also accommodated cyclists, presumably for bed and breakfast. At the rear of the pub was one of Meopham's public wells which was closed off in 1907 and filled in at some point during 1919. In recent years, the old Fox and Hounds pub closed, was transformed and reopened in 2002/3 as a restaurant called Bartellas shown in the recent picture.

This 1935 picture shows the junction of Huntingfield Road, off to the west, and Wrotham Road, originally known as Camer Corner. Huntingfield Road was possibly named because Mr Allan Smith-Masters kept a kennel of hounds at Camer, and according to Golding-Bird, see page 52, during the period 1760 to 1790 the Huntsman's name was Henry Beven. Both pictures show the semi-detached houses named St David and Shirley but the recent photograph indicates the extent of the Wrotham Road widening.

Camer House (pronounced as 'Kammer') was the seat of the Smith-Masters family, for many years the largest land owner in Meopham. The present building is Georgian, but like many more in the parish, stands on the site of a very much older house. John le Maistre lived here in the thirteenth century. This picture is dated 1887. In those days before the creation of parish councils the celebration of such events as royal jubilees fell to the occupants of the big house to organise. Here we see the band formed up before Camer House, ready to process through the village on the occasion of Queen Victoria's Golden Jubilee. The uniform of the bandsmen, with their distinctive pillbox hats, has not been positively identified, but by reference to the badges of rank which some are wearing, they may have come from the Royal Engineers at Chatham. The house itself has changed little, except that the creeper has been cut down as can be seen in the later photograph.

Camer Parade was developed as the main shopping area of the village in 1946. Initially there were only five shops but those north of the China Palace restaurant were added later as were those above the fish and chip shop, as far as Longfield Road. The gabled house in the earlier picture bore a notice advertising properties for sale, those lying between the parade and Huntingfield Road, at £495 and above. The parade is now a busy retail area and parking facilities have been improved at the forefront of the shops. Due to the volume of traffic now travelling the Wrotham Road, and the presence of two schools at the top of Longfield Hill, a road island and railings have been placed to aid the safety of pedestrians.

The position of Meopham Court, so near the church, suggests very strongly that this site was originally the residence of the ancient Saxon chief of the village. Also known as Court Lodge, it would have been the centre of the village organisation in Meapa's time as well as functioning as a farm. This manor was owned by Christchurch, Canterbury resulting from a bequest from Byrhtric, who was Lord of the Manor in the late tenth century, and served as a retirement home and hospital for the diocesan clergy. The court was bought by a Robert Barnett in 1852 and he altered it to its present appearance in the 1860s. The pictures show mainly the Georgian part of the house whereas the Elizabethan section is to the left hand side. Eventually the house was sold off to wealthy lay owners and the last sale was in February 1949, when the Lordship of the Manor including the freehold of the village greens was sold to the parish council for £25.

The Sarsen stone, originally situated outside the churchyard wall (on the old picture), was moved inside the wall during the widening of the Wrotham Road (on the new picture). These stones are of sandstone from the tertiary geological period and the name 'Sarsen' is thought to be a corruption of 'Saracen' due to the ancient belief that the stones are petrified Saracens. The widening of the Wrotham Road in the 1960s necessitated the removal of the beautiful chestnut trees that can be seen lining the road in the earlier photograph.

This picture is taken from an engraving showing the north-east aspect of the church of St John the Baptist in the eighteenth century. Built in 1325 to replace an earlier structure, the church tower was hardly higher than the roof-ridge of the nave. The tower was then extended by twenty feet in 1837 to accommodate a bell chamber at a cost of £215. This work was finished off with battlements as shown in the modern picture.

This view of the inside of the church from the east shows the fifteenth-century font in the foreground. Since the old picture was taken, the church has undergone a major refurbishment in which a new floor has been installed and the Victorian pews replaced by more versatile stackable chairs seen in the recent picture.

The St John's church choir of the 1960s is pictured outside the church with the incumbent choirmaster, John Preston Bell. The modern picture shows the choir in 1995 with a much younger choirmaster.

The post office serving the Meopham church area was for a time before the First World War located in an annex to Church Cottages. The delivery staff are here seen posed outside the premises, wearing the distinctive post office hats with brims back and front. The bicycle on the right appears to have been a post office issue, with its rack for the mailbags, whereas the one used by the young man on the left has no such attachment. It was probably his own property. The postman on the extreme left is Mr 'Batty' Stevens, a prominent member of the Meopham Cricket Club. A wide selection of postcards was on sale, as well as cigarettes and the usual sundry items found to this day in similar establishments. The telephone exchange was in the room behind the window on the left, and this may well have accounted for the bricked-up doorway. To the extreme right of the picture is part of another building, and this was, until 1899, the Meopham Cycle Works. The modern photograph now shows the Church Cottages as private residences.

This rather deceptive view of the road junction of Wrotham Road and Shipley Hills Lane dates to the early years of this century. There was a wide entrance to the lane, with a common triangle of grass. In 1917 the parish council acquired an acre of land on the west side of Wrotham Road for a burial ground, and duly enclosed it. In doing so the wall was built to form a tight right angle, enclosing the green and part of the road! This caused a serious traffic hazard in later years, which was not rectified until the 1970s. The vicarage stands on the site of an earlier building, and dates from about 1865. It was sold in 1950 and the rector, Vernon Nicholls reported 'what a joy it was to be free of cold draughts and to move into a new, warm vicarage'. In 1952 it became the private home of Arthur Skeffington MP and his wife Sheila, who was instrumental in introducing the school for autistic children in Longfield Road. After the MP's premature death in 1971 the house was partially demolished and a new wing added, strictly in keeping with the style of the original, to form a very attractive group of flats. The flint wall was demolished to accommodate the road widening but rebuilt to exactly match the original. The new vicarage was erected to the rear on what was part of the glebe land.

These two pictures show the frontage of the old vicarage, before and after the new wing was added in 1971.

The parish has had as many as six post offices in operation at the same time, although in each case they have tended to move to different premises in the particular locality. This picture shows the office in The Street, where it was still located in 1986. For a time it left these premises (Elizabeth House) and moved to Church Cottages (see page 32). Apart from normal post office business, the shop was clearly selling a range of grocery and other household goods. There are advertisements for Hudson's Soap and Peek, Frean & Co Biscuits. Several of the well-known biscuit tins can be seen stacked inside the right-hand window. The left-hand window carries what appears to be an advertisement for emigration to Canada. The ladies on the steps are probably members of the Clarke family and the addition of the words 'Telegraph Office' above the sign suggests that this part of the post office service had been newly provided. Security reasons dictated the bricking-up of the cellar accesses, and the letterbox first relocated to the wall (page 36) was then removed. Elizabeth House is now a private residence.

These pictures show Elizabeth House with and without the letterbox located in the wall of the house. Apart from its function as a post office, this surprisingly large timber-framed house served as a parish workhouse from 1724 to 1834 and records show that there were twenty inmates present during the latter year.

The George Inn, unquestionably the oldest public house in the village, was formerly called the Market Crouche (i.e. Cross), a reminder that the village market was held weekly in the road outside and in The Street opposite. This picture dates to about 1890, when Samuel Meakin was the licensee, and shows very well the leisurely pace of life at that time. The driver of the baker's cart was no doubt inside the house enjoying a drink, and he had no qualms about leaving his vehicle on the main road through the village. On the left-hand wall are two windows bricked-up to avoid the hated window tax. Both of them have been opened up again. The famous Stock Trees are in full leaf in the centre of the picture. On the right can be seen the corner of Well House, so named because it has a deep well adjacent to the kitchen, from which the villagers were allowed to draw water in the days before the piped supply. The Stock Trees are no longer there, as seen in the modern picture, casualties of the necessary road widening process.

The George Inn an Old Stock Trees, Meopham.

This picture was taken from the Well House corner of the road junction, the site occupied many years ago by the market cross, and looking to the south. The construction of the George Inn in two parts can clearly be seen, with the older part nearer the camera. From the absence of leaves on the famous Stock Trees, it is certainly a winter view. The Stock Trees were planted on the site of the old village stocks, where malefactors were punished in full view of those attending the market. The motorcar has stopped for petrol at the filling station built on the site of former Dodmore House. The hedge beyond the George has now gone and the field behind it is occupied with housing. It was to the right of the telephone pole that a Roman farmstead was discovered. The pole is carrying six or seven pairs of wires, showing the few subscribers in the south end of the village in the 1920s. The modern picture, again, shows the absence of the Stock Trees and the contrasting width of the Wrotham Road.

Meopham School.

Meopham School, built in 1841, was constructed on a site sold to St John's church by the Dean and Chapter of Canterbury at a cost of £149 9s raised by subscription in the village. In the picture, a cross can be seen by the roof apex beneath the pair of chimneys which had the dual function as a bell tower. The later picture shows how modern buildings have replaced the old ones.

Until 1912 Meopham had no purpose built village hall, and social gatherings were held in rooms, sheds and some of the public houses. This changed in 1912, when the village hall, here seen just after completion was built at a cost of nearly £2,000 by a local benefactor. He was Edward Robert Pacey Moon, MP, who had not long before bought Green Farm as his residence. He was member for St. Pancras North. The land on which the hall stands was bought from the Gravesend Land Company. The hedge along Wrotham Road, as well as the trees beside the drive, is very newly planted. In its original form the hall consisted of the main hall, complete with the stage, a committee room, kitchen and dressing room behind. There must have been some form of heating as a chimney stack is visible. Now, extended and modernised the hall has become a very active venue for the many clubs and societies that use its premises.

This picture of the interior of the village hall can be dated to the period about 1927, some fifteen years after the hall had been built. It shows the quite interesting architectural methods used by Lord Ferrers, the architect appointed by Edward Moon. The provision of a stage was a great boon to the village, and the ability of various organisations to put on theatrical productions was instrumental in bringing about a great change in the cultural development of the village. The hall had to be lit by lamps, as electricity did not come to Meopham until about 1930. Several lamps can be seen in the picture. One of the first projects of the Women's Institute after its formation in 1923 was to raise funds to provide equipment for the village hall. The provenance of the grand piano on stage is not known, but now just an upright piano has been provided. The flourishing dramatic group, known as the Meopham Players, regularly show splendid productions using these facilities. The modern picture shows how the hall is also used for horticultural shows and exhibitions.

Kent Terrace, built in 1867, is situated just north of Meopham Green on the east side of Wrotham Road. At No 1 a Mrs Caller used to have a small village shop during the Second World War, while her husband operated a coal business. Note the change in shape of the green after road widening.

At least six forges are known to have been operated in Meopham at different times. This one stood on the east side of Meopham Green, and was at the time of this picture (about 1912) operated by the Dalton family. The bungalow behind the workshop is still there, and bears the name The Old Forge. The smithy and the workshop have gone. The traditional chestnut tree was fairly young then, but is still growing today. A clutter of agricultural machinery can be seen in front of the workshop. Wheelwrighting was an essential part of the smith's business and he had the tyring stone under the tree where it still can be found. As can be seen by the recent photograph, the forge is now residential.

Unveiling Ceremony, War Memorial, Meopham.

The Meopham War Memorial was a subject of much debate in the parish in the years after 1918. Various proposed memorials were considered by the committee set up for the purpose, and most were discarded on the grounds of cost. The design was finally approved, and construction put in hand. The memorial was finally unveiled and dedicated on 23 October 1920, after eighteen months of deliberations. By this time only £186 had been raised towards the cost, and the minute book does not record how or whether the remainder of the cost was met. Behind the memorial is the Green Farm oast and barn, a reminder of the importance of hop growing in earlier years. In the modern picture the mature trees hide the oast which is still in the same position as in the older picture.

This view of the west side of Meopham Green was taken about 1904, and shows the newly erected drinking fountain. An interesting feature is the wire protection around the trees and bushes. The trees were planted in commemoration of the diamond jubilee of Queen Victoria (1897) and are now quite mature. Of the bushes there is no trace or remembrance. The green in those days was under the control of the Church Commissioners, as Lords of the Manor, and it is no doubt their notice board within the wires. On the far side of the road is one of the milestones erected by the Turnpike Trust in 1827. In the far corner of the green, horses are quietly grazing undisturbed by any traffic. The telephone poles carry just one pair of wires, serving Leylands, half a mile to the south. The recent photograph shows the existence of Pitfield Drive, opposite the fountain on the western side of the Wrotham Road, constructed in 1956.

The drinking fountain on Meopham Green was erected by the parish council in 1903 to commemorate the coronation of King Edward VII in the previous year. It cost £75, towards which a contribution of £25 was received from the Metropolitan Drinking Fountain Association. Apart from providing for human visitors, there was a tap from which water could be drawn for horses and cattle, and there was also a trough at ground level for dogs. The picture, from 1908, shows the use to which the facility was put by carters. The horse on the left is about to enjoy his drink, while the other waits patiently. In the background is the Green Farm oast and barn. The oast survived for several more years as part of a new dwelling, but sadly the barn was structurally beyond conversion and had to be demolished. Nevertheless the tiles were salvaged and used for hanging on the new building. The little girl with her governess and the dog is May Russell. Her mother, Bertha Russell, who owned the emporium at the corner of the green, used various members of her family to pose for photographs which, when converted into postcards sold well in the village. The recent photograph indicates the juxtaposition of the fountain and memorial.

This view of the north end of Meopham Green pre-dates the First World War, and shows some of the substantial development that had already taken place there. On the left is Dashwood Court, with a brick wall next to it. At the end of the wall is a field gate, a relic of the farm which used to occupy the area. The gate has gone and the drive leads to a small factory where Mr and Mrs Sherwin, owners of Dashwood Court, produced and sold their own brand of window cleaning cream. Their deaf son, Roland, was an accomplished artist. Next come two pairs of villas (Sunnyside), and to the right of them is another relic of the farm, a large barn with its centre doors leading directly onto the main road. At that time the land behind all these buildings was still agricultural, and included a large orchard. The barn was taken down about 1955 to allow the erection of a new dwelling for the owner of the butcher's shop standing next to it. By that time the back land had been disposed of for the building of Cricketers Drive. After the war the village War Memorial was erected on the green in the centre of the picture. The recent picture shows how parts of the Green have been sacrificed in order to widen the roads.

This picture of Green Farm dates back to 1907 which, when compared with the more recent photograph has shown few external changes apart from the extension on the left. If one refers to the index of the parish map of 1864, the area in which this farm is to be found is called 'The Small Hamlet of Pitfield' and yet now it is the largest and most important part of Meopham, as its centre previously known as Pitfield Green, is now Meopham Green. It seems that Pitfield owes its name to the previous existence of pits from which loam was removed.

Green Farm Cottages stand on the east side of Meopham Green, and were built to provide accommodation for the farm workers on the adjacent farm. This shows them some time before 1914, when they stood alone along that part of the green. The cottages have now been painted, as shown in the recent picture, but otherwise have altered little. The large tree to their right has gone, and modern houses now stand there. To the right of the picture is Mr W Tickle the farmer at Lomer Farm, with his horse-drawn milk float. Carts like this were the usual means of delivering milk in both town and country. His assistant stands at the cottage gate with a small churn. There was no bottling then as milk was measured and poured straight into whatever receptacle was handy. The children and their dog belong to the Russell family. With the growth of motor traffic, the parish council has had to put posts around the green to protect it.

This picture shows the old Pitfield farm house, built in 1801 (the same year as the windmill), and later called Pitfield Cottage. It stood at the south-east corner of Pitfield Green. It was a fairly substantial building, under a slate roof, and the owners enjoyed good views –from the front rooms across the green, and from the back across Happy Valley to David Street and Harvel. To the left is the very substantial barn of traditional construction. The farm extended to about 60 acres. Dr Golding-Bird bought Pitfield Cottage as a holiday home in 1894 after the death of the previous owner, Dr Baber, his father-in-law. He and his wife lived there until 1897 when it was pulled down and Pitfield House was erected on the site of the cottage and the barn. Pitfield House then became the home of Mr and Mrs Alexander but has since been pulled down and replaced by several contemporary detached houses as shown in the modern picture. During the demolition of the house a pike-head with a ten-inch blade was discovered and in the kitchen garden (which had formerly been part of the village green) a silver groat of Henry VIII, a silver penny of Henry III and two more recent copper coins were unearthed.

Pitfield Cottage, Meopham

This picture described as Pitfield Cottage is in fact of Pitfield House, the mansion built on the site of the former barn of Pitfield Farm (see page 50). It was named after Pitfield Green, so called from the loam pits which had been dug there over the centuries. There is indeed a reference in a document of 1306 to 'Pettesfield'. We see the attractive wrought iron gates protecting the entrance and behind them is a belt of trees, one of which is the mulberry tree said to have been planted by the famous gardener, John Tradescant. The tree is still there, although now somewhat decrepit. The road leading off to the left, now known as Steeles Lane, is the old road to Ryarsh, gated at that point and was once one of the original carriage routes from Trosley Towers to the station. This was one of several roads that the parish was able to get removed from its maintenance responsibility in 1871. The later picture shows little of the building due to the thick foliage.

This picture shows Pitfield House when it was occupied by Dr Cuthbert Hilton Golding-Bird, the author of a comprehensive book entitled *The History of Meopham* published in 1934. Golding-Bird was born in London in 1848, the fourth son of an eminent physician. Young Golding-Bird was educated at Tonbridge and at King's College, London and began his medical training at Guy's Hospital, he was eventually appointed Full Surgeon there in 1893. On retirement he came to live in Pitfield Cottage as a holiday home, in Meopham, it was pulled down in 1897 and Pitfield House erected on the site of the old barn. This became his home until his death in 1939. The recent picture shows how much has changed.

This view of the south-west corner of Meopham Green dates from the early years of the twentieth century. Mrs Bertha Russell, a member of a family still to be found in the parish, kept a large emporium stocking clothing, boots, china, toys, glass, millinery, drapery and many other lines. This indicates how the village was very much more self-sufficient in shopping matters than it is today; and that at a time when the population was a mere fraction of the present one. Next to Russell's is the Kings Arms (originally called the Smith's Arms, the name being changed just after the restoration of the monarchy in 1660). The building without doubt dates back to the seventeenth century, and quite possibly earlier. A baker's delivery cart has been left standing outside the public house, and the horse bus to Gravesend is waiting in front of the mill. The recent photograph shows how the shop is now a private residence and the road around the Green has become a car park.

This view of the south-west corner of Meopham Green is somewhat later than the previous picture. What had been Russell's clothing and boot stores was then taken into use as a private residence. The former china, glass and toys department remained in commercial use, and was let to Norton Brothers for use as a cycle shop. They have displayed a cycle wheel on the corner of the building as their trade sign. Their tenancy was almost certainly on a lock-up basis, as the upper floor has identical curtains at each window, and they seem to match those hanging at the ground floor windows. It is interesting to note that at some later time this building reverted to full business use, selling grocery, and acting as a post office. The cycle shop was later a bank and a cafe, but the whole of the premises is once again a private house as shown in the recent picture.

The centre of the picture shows the former Parish Black Cottages, lying between Wellington Cottages and the stores. They were of wooden construction, timber clad, and treated with tar for weather protection. They had thatched roofs. The one on the right was occupied by Mr R Goodwin. His fascia board above the door read 'Splint Maker and Thatcher'. He can be seen sitting outside, with his wife in the doorway. In later years he went blind, but managed to earn a living by turning the handle of a large mangle. His wife took in mangling from local families, who thus avoided the need for ironing their washing. Across the road stands the mill, with its cluster of shops. On the left, half glazed, is the tea –room, with a brick store behind it, and while on the right is the corn and feed shop. All these have now gone, but one small shop, which served as a TV repair service, survived for a few years before it too had to close. The modern picture depicts the contemporary style house that replaced the Black Cottages.

The horse bus, owned and driven by Mr Joseph Clark, has just completed its journey from Gravesend on this occasion pulled by a single horse. The goods piled onto the roof show very clearly its function as a vehicle carrying freight as well as passengers. The timetable of the late 1890s shows that he operated a journey to Gravesend at 6.30 am on Monday, Wednesday, Friday and Saturday, returning thence at 1.30 p.m. There was an extra trip on Saturday evening at 6.15 p.m., returning at 9.30 p.m. A second service ran from Meopham church to Gravesend via Cobham, at 9.15 a.m. on Monday and Thursday, returning at 2 p.m. The single fare was six pence, a considerable sum out of the wages then earned. In the background is Mill House and, to the right, Cosy Cottage, then a grocery shop. The recent picture shows how much reliance is now placed on motors.

Ye olde Windmill, Meopham

The windmill, built about 1801 by the Killick family from Strood, was the last of at least eight known to have existed in the parish from the seventeenth century onwards. It is a smock mill, standing on a massive brick base, and is here seen as it was in the early twentieth century. At that time it carried two pairs of millstones, driven by wind power alone. About 1923, a third pair was added, and a gas engine was provided to supplement the power on days with little or no wind. The mill remained in the ownership of the Killick family until about 1895, when it was sold to the Nortons, another well-known Kentish milling family. That family had it until the last miller, Mr Leslie Norton, died in 1967. A trust was then set up to take over and restore the mill from the very derelict condition into which it had declined, and this has been achieved as can be seen in the recent photograph.

57

This picture shows the Mr Norton working on the millstone inside the mill, a part of the ground floor of the mill has now become the Parish Council office. The recent picture shows the office with, in anticlockwise order, Councillor Barbara Wade (Vice Chairman), Councillor Douglas Powell (Chairman), councillors Sheila Buchanan, Max Bramer and Deputy Clerk Sarah Steven.

The Cricketers Inn, Meopham.

This picture, probably dating from the late 1920s, shows the windmill in a condition of some dereliction with two of the sails blown off, and with the shutters and the vanes of the fantail all missing. After 1923 the mill was worked by a gas engine which had been brought from a mill at Boughton near Faversham. The shop, earlier the Meopham Clothing and Boot Stores became the Meopham Cash Stores, but was eventually demolished and the next owners of the house converted the front exterior into a general store. Sadly this did not last and the next owners demolished the whole house and built a large contemporary dwelling quite out of keeping with the other buildings at the Green, totally obscuring the very attractive Mill House next door. The Cricketers is seen in the fairly short-lived garb of trellis work decoration. The left-hand doorway had been put in, but neither of the porches had been provided. The lamp on the left-hand corner of the house suggests that electricity had been installed. At first floor level, on the right-hand section, can be seen the Automobile Association roundel for Meopham. The lower part gives the information 'Gravesend 6' and a mileage to London, the latter too small to read. The roundel was a casualty of the Second World War. The recent picture shows the result of the Cash Stores building replacement as well as the changes to the façade of the Cricketers Inn.

Gallant All-night Battle to Save a Windmill

This is a copy of a press cutting which describes an incident in which Mr W. M. Norton (erroneously named Morton) and his sons Leslie and David risked their lives on top of Meopham's windmill in a night-time fight to save it from collapse during a storm. Unfortunately two sails were lost, but the mill was saved. William Norton died in 1951 and left the mill to Leslie, as his heir, who continued to run the mill for a few years during a period of declining trade. Eventually, he struck a deal with Kent County Council and sold the mill for a token sum, along with the hexagon of land on which it stands, to the KCC. A trust has since been set up jointly by the Meopham Parish Council and the Meopham Windmill Society.

This picture shows a meeting of the West Kent Hunt in front of the Cricketers Inn. This public house has been known, over the years, as 'The Cricketers Arms', 'The Eleven Cricketers' and more recently but thankfully for a brief while only 'The Long Hop'. Since then it has changed hands several times and now houses a large rear extension as additional restaurant space.

The private residence now called Basque Cottage, on the north side of the Cricketers Inn, was originally a public house in 1712 called 'The Swan', the bar being in the downstairs room on the left of the picture. The pub was licensed by Thomas Romney and became the birthplace of the famous Kent cricketing son, Valentine. In 1728 it changed its name to 'The Harrow', but from 1735 to 1765 it was known as 'The Eleven Cricketers'. Richard Buggs became the new licensee in 1765 and for the next hundred years the Buggs family was associated with the inn. Basque Cottage was at one time the Headquarters of the Meopham Cricket Club.

Richard Buggs, the licensee of the Eleven Cricketers in the premises now known as Basque Cottage needed larger premises, but not until 1790 was he able to build on adjoining land which he bought from a neighbouring farmer. This building became what is now known as the old section of 'The Cricketers Inn'. Richard's grandson, Henry, extended it, in the 1820s, to provide a club room and his own accommodation. This extension can be seen clearly in both 'Then' and 'Now' pictures. Arthur Jones, the licensee whose name appears on the sign in the old picture of the Cricketers Inn, held the licence from 1907 to 1915 and was succeeded by his wife Loisa. The recent picture shows the modern appearance of the inn.

The top photograph shows the old cricket pavilion, dating from 1920, which was extended to include changing rooms in 1932, and had a further extension in 1961 for the addition of a balcony and scorebox. The recent photograph shows the new pavilion built after 1985. Apart from the changing rooms, toilet, and bar, this new pavilion also has also a roomy, comfortable, meeting room, often used by parish sub-committees.

This picture shows the cricketers by the cricket pavilion in 1927 with a similar picture of 2012 cricketers. The Meopham Cricket Club commemorated its bicentenary in 1976, although they could even have celebrated it earlier as the earliest reference to cricket on the green was in 1773 and the 'Eleven Cricketers' public house, originally in Basque Cottage as it is now called, dates back to 1712. Meopham Green (originally Pitfield Green) is one of the best in Kent and this, of course, is due to the Cricket Club management, especially when one realises how open it is to the public and has been used for rallies as well as sports other than cricket.

This is a picture of cricket on the Green taken from the top of Meopham Mill in about 1946. The roof of the Cricketers Inn can be seen clearly in the foreground, and across the Green, the barn built by Bill Russell, just after the Second World War, to replace the one demolished by the V-1 pilotless plane (doodlebug). A game of cricket is in progress and spectators' cars are parked around the edge of the Green. The recent photograph was also taken in a north easterly direction from the top of the Mill.

Here we have a picture of the detached two storey house, Meopham Lodge, built in 1851 and at one time known as Meopham Villa, previously owned by William James J. Buggs who also owned Wellington Cottages and the Cricketers Inn.

Norway House is now the Head Office and shop of The Meopham Valley Vineyard as can be seen in the 'Now' picture. The 'Then' picture shows the barn and yard being used by an undertaker, J. Durling, who also offered a building and plumbing service. The date of the photograph is unknown, but probably *c.* 1899. In 1950, Woodhead and Cuff used the premises to run a car hire business, and by 1959 Malcolm Cuff had expanded his interests into timber, plywood and hardboard. In 1981, Ken Hawkins founded 'The Press on the Green' which operated until he retired in 1995.

This timber-framed house known as Barnside, was originally a farmhouse. Over the years it has functioned as a Butcher, originally owned by Mr Chinnery, who passed the business on to Gilbert Holmes, who after the First World War sold the business to Oliver Russell. Mr Russell ran the butcher shop until 1951, then sold it to Cyril King. When Mr King's business closed down, Barnside became an antique shop and now it functions as a cattery.

Greenfields is a wooden residential building, at present on the eastern side of Wrotham Road, just south of the Green. Built in the 1820s, it was originally situated on the opposite side of the road, behind the Mount Zion Baptist Church, in what is now the car park where it is thought to have functioned as a Manse. In the 1890s, having no concrete foundation, it was dismantled and transferred across the road to its present position on the east side, as shown in the older photograph, where it was probably used as a Sunday school. The recent photograph shows how little the building's appearance has changed over the years.

Mount Zion Baptist Church and the terrace of four houses beyond, named 'Lily Cottage', 'Danescote', 'Hartsdown' and 'Fern Villa' in the part of the Wrotham Road which used to be called 'Leading Street'. The recent picture shows clearly how the road has been widened, the surface improved and how much of the vegetation has been removed to facilitate it.

Leading Street is that part of the Gravesend to Wrotham Road between Meopham Green and South Street. The name has tended to drop out of use in these days of post codes. This view, another of those published by Mr W. Parsons, shows the terrace of twentieth century houses (Kathlie, Gordon and Boyland Cottages) built on the east side of the road in the early part of this century. Further development in more recent years has led to the loss of the mature trees on the road side beyond the houses, the loss of the hedge on the right, and the widening of the road itself. The gate and stile leading to Steeles Lane can just be seen at the bend in the road in the older picture, but the lane has now been opened up for traffic to allow access to buildings further up the lane.

Kilarney was for many years a small retirement home the proprietor of which was Rosemary Sutehall. The 'Then' picture probably predates the retirement home showing the probable residential owner Mrs OBrian. Now the extended building houses the local Veterinary Surgeon's practice.

Cherry Hay is now a private house, standing on the east side of Wrotham Road, but it was built as a public house known as 'The Prince of Wales' in 1847. This house, constructed of flint and brick, was built to replace a much older pub, known as 'The Coffin', which stood further back from the road and of which there is little evidence now. The Coffin, dated from 1715, has been described as a low pitched building, with a thatched roof, lying back from the road with a small green in front. The inn sign stood on the green and showed the effigy of a coffin, although some reports suggest that the pub was originally called 'The Cradle and Coffin'. The Coffin's replacement, The Prince of Wales, was built between the old building and the road by the then licensee, Thomas Goodwin, although it had an active life as a pub for only forty years as the premises were sold to a Dr Baber for conversion into a private house in 1887. Appearances of both new and old photographs are very similar so there must be few external changes.

The first Baptist Church in Meopham, Mount Zion, was built on Leading Street in 1828, and this continued to serve the congregation until 1927. In that year, due to a doctrinal difference, some of them decided that a separate church would better suit their spiritual needs. A plot of land at South Street was obtained from the late Thomas Day, a member of the church, and on it the South Street Baptist Church was built, by voluntary labour. This picture shows the then new church when it was almost complete. It was a timber-framed building, clad with asbestos sheeting. The church was consecrated on 1 November 1928 by Pastor John Monroe of Eynsford Baptist Church. Tea was served at 5 p.m., at a charge of sixpence each! The building continued in use until 1983, in which year it was demolished and the present church replaced it. Its present appearance can be seen in the recent photograph.

The Boy Scouts' camping ground at Hope Hill on the eastern side of Wrotham Road, just north of Culverstone was purchased in 1950. The local Association had begun collecting funds to purchase a site some twenty-five years previously, but it was only when it received a legacy of £2,008 from Walter Matthews, purchase was able to proceed. The amenity block shown here is known as The Clifford Allen Centre, after a legacy was bequeathed by the family of its namesake who spent many happy camping hours as a boy in the 1920s. The centre is a multi-roomed training and accommodation building in which all the facilities are suitable for disabled users. At Hope Hill, emphasis has been on adventurous activities and this has attracted thousands of visitors a year to Meopham from all parts of the world. Not all the visitors are Scouts, many are from youth groups and societies, art classes and history clubs but all are made very welcome.

The site has its own chapel and the pictures here show how the temporary Chapel Gate has been replaced by a less rustic construction.

The correct name of this property (here wrongly described as South Street House) is South House, and it used to be a public house, owned by two brothers named Loft, it was then known as 'The Two Brewers'. In its early days it was a farmhouse owned by James Loft. He opened it as a pub in 1839, no doubt to benefit from the increased traffic which it was expected would use the road after it had been improved by the Turnpike Trust. The farming, mainly market gardening, continued, and the licensed business was conducted in the room on the right of the picture. Entrance to this room was by a door in the end wall, now closed up. The beer cellar was beneath that room, and the cellar flap is clearly visible below the window. This picture was taken soon after the beer business had ceased. The beer house closed and this house once again became a family home. A highly successful nursery was developed by the Cleggett family at the rear of the property and a plant and preserves shop opened in the old barn facing the road. After many years, resulting from severe winters and drought ridden summers it was decided to close the nursery. The barn was reconstructed to form a family house for Pam Cleggett, her mother and father and the original South House was put on the market as a separate dwelling as shown in the recent picture. South House stands on the west side of Wrotham Road, just north of Culverstone School and its appearance now is shown in the recent photograph.

Owls Castle is a sixteenth-century timber-framed house which is listed, but the picture is that of the barn which is of a similar date. Originally known as Cook's Farm after the owner's family, the curious name 'Owls' Castle' was not acquired until the 1861 census. The property has changed hands many times during the centuries and details can be found in Jim Carley's *History of Culverstone*. The present occupant is the caterer "Just Sara" and the refurbished barn shown in the recent picture makes a splendid banqueting hall.

This rare picture of Culverstone old school dates back to the early years of this century. The school, standing on the east side of Wrotham Road, was built in 1872, on land given by Mr Amos Fletcher, to serve the growing area of that part of the parish. It served as both church and school. The main part of the building was used as a church and doubled as a classroom for the older pupils. The vestry doubled as a room for the younger ones, and for hanging up their coats. A new and larger school was built across the road in 1959, although the old one continued in use for a few years more. Plans were made for it to become a community centre, but did not materialise and it was demolished. The school house, in similar style, still stands in Whitepost Lane, as seen in the recent picture, and is now a private residence as seen in the recent picture, but sadly the old school bell which hung above the school house disappeared mysteriously and has never been recovered.

In 1924 Charles Cook began business on the west side of Wrotham Road on the site of the present Texaco garage at Culverstone. He started with a shed, as can be seen in the picture, as a cycle repair business. He was later joined by his brother Roland and they branched out into gramophones, early wireless sets, cycle manufacture and the sale of petrol. In 1931 they bought a lorry for Roland to transport farm produce enabling Charles to concentrate on the retail side of the business which expanded into the repair of cars and tractors. In 1953, Charles moved across the road into larger premises and became a thriving business catering for all household and gardening needs. The site is now occupied by 'Costcutter' which is where the original 'sole' or pond, was situated, from which Culverstone (in a 1381 document, Culver sole, as Culverstone was then named), can be translated to 'a muddy pond frequented by doves'. The recent picture shows the site of the original Cooks' shop which is now a Texaco garage.

Culverstone Green is one of the smallest of Meopham's seven greens, has changed little over the years, and consisted of a strip of grassland and a small pond on the eastern side of Wrotham Road. As seen in the recent picture, the pond has now disappeared and the green is narrower after the main road was widened. Behind the green to the east is a large field, now a recreation ground, which was a racecourse organised for a few years in the late nineteenth-century by a local bookie named Meadows.)

Lindenwood was an eighteen-roomed mansion house, with domestic servants, built between 1850 and 1860 on a four acre site with stables, tennis courts, and a worker's cottage. It was occupied by the Demedewe family until 1966 when a nephew Edwin Everett became resident until he died in 2012 when the mansion was demolished. The recent picture shows the site after Lindenwood has been demolished and shows the construction of new buildings.

Millers Farm is situated right at the south end of the village, alongside the Gravesend to Wrotham Road. It was later renamed as Tower Grange, and is now generally called Tower Folly. In years gone by one of its principal crops was the growing of hops, and sufficient were grown to justify the provision of their own oast, dating from the nineteenth century. Unlike many in the village this has been converted for residential use with the addition of dormer windows. With the road widening scheme of a few years ago, the very rural appearance which is such a feature of this picture, has been lost, particularly with the loss of the trees on the west (Stanstead) side of the road. This picture was one of a series published by Mr W. Parsons, who kept the village stores at Meopham Green. His somewhat archaic spelling was no doubt intended to give a sense of antiquity to the view. The recent picture shows how the building is kept in good repair.

The Vigo Inn is just outside the parish boundary, but it serves as a local for both Culverstone and the Vigo Village, to which it gave its name. Originally called The Upper Drover, an indication that some of the trade would have come from the time when sheep and cattle were taken to market and pasture on the hoof. The building may date as far back as 1471 and is likely to have changed its name because of the Battle of Vigo during the war of the Spanish Succession in 1702. The story tells that the life of the Fleet Commander, Admiral Sir George Rooke, was saved by a sailor who lived locally. At the end of hostilities, the pub was bought for the sailor and renamed Vigo in recognition of his bravery. Modernisation took place in 1950 leaving only the large open fireplace in the saloon as part of the original building and the external view can be seen in the 'now' photograph. The Vigo is the home of a table skittles game known as 'Daddlums'.

The Trosley Towers picture shows how the mansion looked in its heyday. It was built in 1885 by Sir Sydney Waterlow who was the chairman of his family firm of printers and a wealthy London benefactor. It cost £250,000 to build and emerged as a splendidly furnished mansion with extensive views across the downs and surrounded by acres of parkland, all immaculately maintained. On his death in 1906, the house and the estate passed to his son, Sir Philip Waterlow. An unfortunate lawsuit concerning fraudulent Portuguese banknotes involved the firm and Sir Philip was obliged to pay considerable compensation despite being innocent of any illegal action. The estate diminished in value and, on his death in 1931, his son and heir, Sir Edgar Waterlow, sold off all the employees' houses and, one year later put the entire estate up for auction. Only in 1935 did the house itself find a buyer, a Mr Shahmoon. In 1936 he arranged for the whole house to be demolished for £2,000. A bare fifty years of existence and this mansion had disappeared. The vegetation of the estate has been allowed to take over. Consequently, to try and find the remaining site is considered dangerous to life and limb due to open cellars, hence the 'Now' picture is of only the gateway to the original driveway.

When the main road from Gravesend to Borough Green, now the A227, was turnpiked by Act of Parliament in 1825, toll houses and gates were erected at appropriate intervals to house the toll collectors. From such rather sparse details as have survived, it is believed that they were all of the same construction. This view is the only known photograph of one such house, in this case located at the Vigo crossroads. Another toll house was situated at the junction of Longfield Road and Wrotham Road, and a third at the point where the modern A2 road crosses Wrotham Road. After their function as toll houses ceased in 1872, the houses continued in use as private dwellings. In turnpike days this house was occupied by Mrs Jeal, who is probably the lady in the picture, and later by Mr and Mrs Oliver. The building eventually fell into a state of disrepair and, like the others, was demolished but the 'now' photograph shows the new bungalow that was built on the site.

White Hill, or Whitehill Road as it is generally called today, links the centre of Meopham with the hamlet of David Street and hence with Harvel. It is a road of considerable antiquity, and over the centuries the surface of the track as it descended the hill was gradually worn away. This left the road in a considerable cutting, and, exposing the chalk, gave the road its name. The process of erosion ceased only when the road surface was covered with tarmacadam in recent years as shown in the 'Now' picture. This view dates to about 1930 and shows the road surface with the wheel tracks on the stone surface, and the distinctive 'trade mark' of horse drawn traffic in the middle. The recent picture shows the metalled road devoid of wheel tracks.

The White Horse public house was built some 300 yards along the Birling Road to the west of the original pub which was burnt down in 1906. However the history of the establishment goes back at least 200 years and was an important port of call for the annual Meopham Beating the Bounds. The parish records show reference to the cost of purchase of food and beer for this event as far back as 1753. The recent photograph shows that the external view of the pub has changed very little but the telegraph pole has leaned a bit more.

Harvel Village Hall was built in 1912 on a site donated by Francis Henry Cripps Day of Holly Hill. Subscriptions were then collected to pay for the construction of the building which was opened in Easter of that year. Welcomed by Harvel residents the premises were used for church services as well as the usual community functions and in 1919, a War Memorial was erected inside to honour those Harvel residents lost during 1914-18 and then extended to include the 1939-45 war. The recent photograph shows the hall as it is today.

Opposite the village hall is a timber-framed building dating from 1590, known as The Forge Cottage, which is the original Amazon and Tiger pub although the sale of beer dates from only 1842. Then the premises were owned by John Roots and were described as a Beer House and Smithy. The forge used to stand to the left of the pub and stayed in business until 1962 when the forge was demolished. The site of the new Amazon and Tiger was bought by the brewers Budden & Briggs in 1913 and the following year they built the new pub to look more like a private house than a public one for fear of causing offence. Thus the Amazon and Tiger is now placed beside the cricket green at Harvel just as Meopham's green is similarly serviced by pubs. The recent picture shows the modern appearance of the Amazon and Tiger public house.

This sunny, summer view of Harvel Street is taken looking east towards the green. At the bottom of the dip is Harvel Pond, with Dene Lane leading off to the left. Just beyond it is the old road cutting across the green, now grassed over. The relocation of this road on the far side of the green has made it a much more attractive feature of the village. The buildings along the street have changed almost completely. The timber-clad house on the left, Pond Farm, remains but has lost its cladding, and has been painted white. The derelict house next to it has been demolished, and a modern house, Little Croft, now stands on the site, although some yards back from the road. The brick wall next to it was the front wall of Forge Cottage, formerly the Amazon and Tiger public house, and this has been replaced with a well-kept yew hedge. On the right, the brick building housed Wallers, a firm that marketed products connected with the use of butane gas but the building has now disappeared and has been replaced by private houses. As shown in the recent photograph, the trees beyond have also gone and their place has been taken by a hedge which has obscured most of the buildings.

This very substantial timber-framed building, known as Barn Cottage, was originally built as a barn on Crickfield Farm, Harvel. The farmhouse is located a few yards to the left of the picture. Early this century the barn, which faces onto Harvel Street, was refurbished and turned into a dwelling house, appropriately called Barn Cottage. It was given a new thatched roof, and a wall was built to separate it from the farm, after which it was sold off from the farm. The roof of thatch was subsequently replaced with traditional Kentish tiles, and the very rural area behind and beside the cottage was gradually turned into a factory making engineering parts of many kinds, but particularly items connected with liquid gas appliances. The walls of the cottage have now been whitened and the exposed timbers stained black. A large modern garage has been built in the garden on the right of the property. Sheds have been put up on the farm side of the wall, which would prevent this view being taken today, however the recent photograph illustrates the picturesque nature of the cottage today.

The Old Pond Farmhouse, which belonged to the McDougall family of flour fame, stands behind the village pond at Harvel and was declared unfit for habitation in the early 1900s. However, it was cleaned up and given a facelift by the Tilley family in 1923. Originally thatched, the thatch was replaced by tiles as a precaution against fire, but then the thatch was restored by the present occupants in 1982.

The ancient manor of Nurstead, originally Nutstead, lies to the north east of Meopham station and although almost impossible to determine its precise age, there is evidence of Roman occupation in that area. Nurstead Court, seen here as an engraving dating from 1838, is an aisled hall house but sadly only about half of the original building remains as the rest was pulled down in the early nineteenth century when the modern façade was built. The surviving part of the house has been calculated to be around from 1320, a date which has been confirmed by tree-ring dating of the roof timbers. This technique gave a range of tree felling dates of from 1299 to 1334. The recent photograph shows how the front façade has changed over the years.

As Nurstead was, at one time, a separate parish, and the parish church (St Mildred's) is about 200 yards south of Nurstead Court. The church is on record in Domesday and it is thought that it existed in the second half of the tenth century. The present building has been extended and modified over the centuries but it most likely dates from the thirteenth century whereas the tower is probably from the fifteenth. Before the bell was installed in the newly built tower it was hung in a nearby tree. The appearance, in the recent picture, is not very different from that of the one taken in the 1930s.